DELIVERED TO GO BEYOND
By Antionette Ware

DELIVERED TO GO BEYOND

Please note: All quotations are taken from the New King James Version (NKJV). All definitions are from Merriam Webster Dictionary.

© 2020 Antionette Ware

All Rights Reserved. No part of this publication may be reproduced or transmitted in any form or by any means, electronic or mechanical, including photocopy, recording, or any information storage and retrieval system, without the prior written permission of the author.

ISBN #: 978-1-735-8828-0-2

Printed in the United States of America.

TABLE OF CONTENTS

ACKNOWLEDGEMENTS

FOREWORD

INTRODUCTION

CHAPTER 1: SPIRIT OF BONDAGE

CHAPTER 2: FOUR LEVELS OF DELIVERANCE

CHAPTER 3: BROUGHT OUT WITH A PURPOSE

CHAPTER 4: IT'S POSSIBLE

CHAPTER 5: I'M GOING IN

DELIVERED TO GO BEYOND

ACKNOWLEDGMENTS

I would like to dedicate this book 1st and foremost to Abba, Father. The Bible says that I didn't choose you, but you chose me and that I was predestined to be a son of God. I am thankful that as a son you, Abba have delivered me and given me the courage and the boldness to follow after my dreams.

To my husband and family for always supporting and undergirding with prayer, my dreams and visions.

Last but not least, to all that have confirmed my dreams through their prophetic voice and all that have helped this project become a reality. I appreciate you!

FOREWORD

We count it a great honor and a privilege to write these words as a foreword to this revealing and exciting book, *"Delivered To Go Beyond."*

Our spiritual daughter in Christ, Prophetess Antionette Ware, has opened her life with transparency and shared many truths that the Holy Spirit has shown her in her journey from defeat to victory. And that is what makes this book relational and applicable.

Delivered To Go Beyond contains patterns upon patterns and prophetic exercises to get you to your destination called breakthrough!

May your life become congruent with the One who sits on the throne, the true bondage breaker, Jesus Christ, as you read and partake in its instructional treasures.

Apostle Rod. L and Prophetess Selena Stevenson, Senior Leaders of Rivers Of Living Water Ministries Int'l. Muskegon, MI

INTRODUCTION

As I prepared to walk into a new year it is usually my custom to seek God for insight. As a prophetic person I know that numbers have meaning and within them lies revelation that I utilize to help navigate through the year 2020. While in preparation and study I begin to seek God for what He wanted to say to His people. The Hebrew Key 2020 *hatstsalah*, means *deliverance*. Immediately when I looked at it, the Holy Spirit spoke and said that this decade will be The Beyond. As I communed with Him, He said, "*I have delivered you to go beyond.*"

The definition of beyond means, *beyond-farther on than, more distant, outside the understanding, limits, or reach of, surpassing*. It also means *to go, to pass, exceed in anything*. Syn- on the other side, over and above, free of."

This is such a powerful definition because most people don't realize how much more God has for us. I can remember growing up as a little girl in the projects. It was an environment that didn't instill in me that I could become more than what I saw on an everyday basis. All I saw was dysfunction, broken families, poverty, addiction, and drug trafficking. I grew up in a time where crack cocaine was becoming more mainstream, leaving a trail of destruction. Somehow, I became convinced that this was how my life was going to be. I couldn't see past where I was, in order to even fathom what God had for me.

In my heart there were things I desired. I wanted a better life, attend college, become a doctor, get married, have a healthy family with children, and travel all over the world. As a child, we lived in a 3-bedroom apartment and I shared a room and a bed with one of my cousins. There were many times when I would just lay on the bed and dream. This bed was white, and the headboard had a space where you could place various things on it. I would write on the headboard the names of places I had desired to visit. But those dreams would fade, and I was convinced it would never be so. Little did I know God had another plan for me that trumped everything else that was happening in my life at the time.

Jeremiah 29:11 says that God knows the plan He has for us. Yes, God has a plan for us but, sometimes we don't see that plan because of the life we are born into. Current situations, circumstances or even our past can keep us from seeing beyond, into the future to what God has for us.

I believe that is why God has given us an imagination. The word *imagination* in the *1828 Websters Dictionary* is *the power or faculty of the mind by which it conceives, and forms ideas of things communicated to it by the organ of sense.* We have five senses and imagination is connected to our sense of sight and perception. The imagination is the thoughts of our heart and where dreams are conceived. Our imagination can be a wonderful thing. It can be a place where we obtain hope even when there is no hope.

We can see things with our eyes that doesn't exist, we can do things that we couldn't do, and we can become the person we want to become, all within our imagination. In the realm of imagination there aren't any restrictions. We have permission to dream as big as we want to. So, the question still remains, why are so many people still living in their current state? The answer is simple. Just like God has a plan for us, so does Satan.

John 10:10 says,

> *"The thief comes only to steal and kill and destroy. I (being Jesus) came that they may have life and have it abundantly."*

Who is the thief? SATAN. Yes, we have a real enemy. Though invisible, his sole purpose is to keep you confined, to steal, kill and destroy every dream you ever had or have. Think about it, have you ever had an idea to do something and you were excited about it but then immediately something in you said *"You can't do that, it's impossible," "You don't have the money", "You don't have the talent,* or *you don't have the skill"*. That's the voice of a stranger coming to keep you stuck where you are, in an effort to make you hopeless, never allowing you to reach God's greatest fulfillment for your life.

Have you ever been in a place where what you have been through or are going through is so hard that you can't see your future, and you've become hopeless?

You are not by yourself. I used to be hopeless, thinking that where I was in that particular moment of my life and after everything I had endured, that I would become the sum total of my life. I couldn't see how my life could ever change. I had lost every expectation of anything good ever happening for me. I still remember the day God infused hope into me and I began to believe that there was more. As I was crying out to Him for deliverance from a state of depression, His Spirit led me to this scripture.

Psalm 42:5

"Why are you cast down, O my soul and why are you in turmoil within me? Hope in God; for I shall again praise him, my salvation."

In that moment I realized that the only person I hadn't put my hope in was God. I realized my hope, and salvation was solely contingent on Him. In that moment, I knew I had to hope again, dream again, and believe again! I had to do something I had not done in a long time, even as a little girl. I had to EXPECT more. Expectation will cause you to look forward to the future with anticipation of all that God has for you!

Listen, if you are in a state of hopelessness, let me encourage you. God's Word is Spirit and Life, and in it and Him is everything you need to go beyond where you are now! It was only God that led me out of captivity into a fruitful place in my life, and He will do the same for you!

As I write this book I'm still growing and maturing but I want to share with you from my own experiences, how God brought me out of bondage to where I am now.

PERSONAL NUGGET

If you are ever going to go beyond you must start! When God shows us our future it can be huge and overwhelming. More than likely we don't know how we are going to accomplish it. If we continue to focus on that it will keep us stagnate. This was my problem I lacked the ability to start, because I was so focused on the finish. The Lord told me to stop focusing on the finish and just start! My problem was just simply mustering up the strength to even start moving toward what He had for me. The word start means to begin, set out, as on a journey or activity. I had to begin, go, move, take action to get on this journey that I am on now. I believe that if you are reading this book it will enable you to start your journey.

Declare, *"This is my start!"*

In this book, I want to help you get past your natural understanding and convince you that on the other side of pain, trauma, dysfunction, poverty, and your past there is more. I will give you practical application that you can use to get from where you are to the place that God has for you! Throughout the book, you will find what I call *Personal Nuggets*. These are specific things that God has said to me at specific times that has helped me to advance, and I pray that they will help you as well. At the end of every chapter, there will be *Power Prayers*, *Power Confessions* or both, that you can utilize by praying and declaring over yourself daily!

My prayer for you is that the eyes of your understanding be enlightened that you may know and see what God has called you to, and what is the immeasurable greatness of His power toward you. That you will surpass any and all limitations that the enemy has tried to place on you and gain the confidence that is needed to reach your fullest potential! That you would know that your current or past situation or circumstances can't stop what God has ordained for you!

CHAPTER 1: THE SPIRIT OF BONDAGE

I have found that in my life and in most people's lives the number one reason we never access the true plan of God for our lives is due to bondage. Whenever I couldn't surpass where I was, I came to realize that there was some type of barrier that was present that kept me from doing so. The Bible describes it as the spirit of bondage.

Romans 8:15

"For you have not received the spirit of bondage again to fear;"

Let's look at and define the two most important words within this scripture, SPIRIT and BONDAGE. Let's look at the word spirit according to the Strong's Exhaustive Concordance.

Spirit H7307- ruwach - breath, wind, rational being, and its expression and function.

Spirit G4151- pneuma - current of air, breath, the rational soul, vital principle for life

There are two kinds of spirits, divine and demonic. This is determined by what the spirit produces. Spirits are the vital principle for life that determine how we feel, think, decide and they influence and inspire our actions and behaviors, whether good or bad. Every spirit needs a body to give expression through. It usually begins with a thought or feeling that will make you make a decision that will influence your actions and behaviors. God's Spirit will cause your soul to be rational hence giving you the ability to make rational decisions.

Demonic spirits will cause your soul to be irrational hence making your behaviors erratic. Simply put, the spirit will either produce righteousness or wickedness. This leads us to the second word, bondage.

Bondage H560-ebed- slave or servant, enslave, to compel to labor or work involuntarily. The state of being bound by or subjected to some external power or control. Physical detention by force.

Syn - confinements, captivity, control, imprisonment, pressure, limitations, chains, hindrance, yoke.

Bondage can be voluntary or involuntary, but the main thing is that it is a giving over of self to some spirit or power.

Exodus 1:1-12 states that the children of Israel went to Egypt in a time of famine but later ended up being enslaved by the Egyptians. Egypt represents *bondage, besiegement, a fortified place, or a place of limitation.* In verse 11 it states that they placed *taskmasters* over them. What is a taskmaster you may ask? *A taskmaster is a person or gang, or a specific spirit that you have given yourself over to or is placed over you to force service or place a burden upon you that will cause you to faint*. It's done through affliction, with the goal to depress and weaken you.

When a person is afflicted it can cause sorrow, grief, fear, restlessness which makes it difficult to enjoy life, pain which could be physical, mental or emotional, and turmoil. When in this state, it can be very difficult to break free.

Most people stay stuck in what has happened to them. They don't ever move past their pain, trauma, or the difficult places in life. When that happens, you have become a slave to what has happened to you. That's called arrested development. You never develop mentally, emotionally or spiritually past that thing that has held you down. When someone is in a state of arrested development, they can't fully come into the fulness of their identity.

Bondage comes to strip you of your identity and will also alter your personality. For me I spent years bound by my past and restricted because of what happened to me. I was arrested in my development and because I didn't have any tools to cope with the things that happened to me, I became this person who God never intended me to be. I became mean, stand offish, turned to drugs, was very depressed and even tried to take my own life.

Another effect of bondage is that you will work, toil and labor, only to produce nothing. This is known as being barren or fruitless. It's like no matter what you do, it doesn't appear that any of your efforts are working and you're not progressing. You're working but you can't seem to get ahead. You save money but then something happens and you're back to nothing. It always feels as if something is hindering you or there's a limitation, barrier or restriction keeping you from coming out of what you're in.

I have shared some of the effects of bondage but let's look at the cause of bondage. A lot of the enslavements that I was experiencing was inherited. It's what we would call generational bondage. This means that there were some things I inherited from my parents. This may be the case for you as well.

Exodus 20:5 says,

> *"Thou shalt not bow down thyself to them, nor serve them: for I the LORD thy God am a jealous God, visiting the iniquity of the fathers upon the children unto the third and fourth generation of them that hate me."*

Bondage is inherited because of the iniquity of the generations before us that we are born into. Iniquity is the result of the failures of our forefathers to do what was right in the sight of the Lord. They failed to teach us because their forefathers failed to teach them. It is the negligence of those responsible for us to teach us how to live right. How do you know if this is what you're dealing with? When you trace your bloodline and all you see is poverty, addiction, abuse, dysfunction or certain patterns and behaviors that most of the people in your family has experienced and you yourself have or is experiencing those things as well, that's iniquity.

Iniquity is rooted in familiar spirits. These are demonic spirits that have access to your bloodline through the negligence of the fathers, in an effort to create a different culture. Culture is the set of shared attitudes, values, goals and practices that characterizes an institution (The family is God's institution). It is our lifestyle or the way of doing things. It is our belief system that when affirmed then creates a behavior.

Most of us have been conditioned to believe that if my parents and grandparents were poor then that's my plight as well. It is a strategy of Satan to create generational bondage by keeping the family bloodline under his influence. The enemy works through iniquity because he doesn't ever want these cycles to be broken. He wants to keep generations of people in bondage. He wants our seeds/children in bondage because if he can get you at the beginning there's a chance, you'll never be free.

The enemy would want you to think that you have no other choice but to stay stuck in the captivity of your bloodline. I want you to know that iniquity can be broken, and you can be delivered. You have to learn how to live aside from the culture/environment that was created for you by your family and God wants to show you how.

God will not hold you accountable for your parent's negligence He will forgive and have mercy but so do you. Forgiveness closes the door to iniquities.

You must forgive their wrongdoing and every injustice that was done against you. Most importantly, you must let go of the need for someone to pay for what happened or was done to you. Don't allow the trespasses and iniquities of you forefathers hold you captive.

Forgiveness will open the door to deliverance, and it will shut the door to all of the effects of bondage. If you have not forgiven, take some time right now to ask God to help you to let go of the pain, trauma, hurt and to give up the right for punishment to come to those that have failed you. Begin to say I forgive (state the person's name) for their negligence and failures to properly care for, nurture and teach me how to live right before the eyes of the Lord. In doing this, I literally heard a door close in the spirit realm and it opened unto me a chance to experience a freedom that I had not experienced before.

It was deliverance that helped me to see beyond where I was and to become who I am today. In order for you to be able to move past these things, you must get delivered. In the book of Exodus, it tells us that the children of Israel cried out to the Lord for deliverance.

Now that you have forgiven, if you have never asked God to deliver you, let's take the time now to ask God to deliver you.

Father, your Word says that you came to set the captive free, and I recognize the need to be set free from everything that has hindered me. I ask that you expose every hidden root system and pull it up by its root. You are a Deliverer, and in You is my freedom. I desire to be free and experience liberation, because where the Spirit of the Lord is there is liberty. Father I ask that you liberate me from all forms of bondage (you can make it personal and add whatever you need to be delivered from) In Jesus name, Amen!

I believe that because you said that prayer your Deliverer has responded as He did to me and the cries of the children of Israel and by the end of this book you will be free and accessing your new!

POWER PRAYER

Father, I thank You that You have not given me the spirit of bondage that would cause me to be fearful. I thank You that you have broken me free from every yoke of bondage. I declare that long term bondages are destroyed now! I am no longer bound by limitations, stagnation, imprisonments, pressure, or any hindrances that would come to confine me and every stubborn obstacle is removed. I decree that Your Spirit is the vital principle for my life, and I am divinely influenced by Your Spirit. I declare I will not voluntarily yield my mind, will or emotions to demonic influences, so that they that will not have expression through my actions and behaviors.

I thank You that I am fortified in You because You are my Fortress and Stronghold! I decree I find my identity in You! I am no longer a slave, but I am a son because of the spirit of adoption! I thank You that every spirit of barrenness is broken off my life. I decree that I am fruitful, productive, and have the capacity to bring forth the life You have for me in Jesus name, Amen!

CHAPTER 2: FOUR LEVELS OF DELIVERANCE

As I stated in the introduction, the Hebrew word *hatstsalah* means *deliverance*. The bible tells us that deliverance is the children bread which means we have a right to freedom and liberation. You don't have to live your life in bondage. You have prayed for deliverance now let's look at what it really means to be free.

To deliver means *to snatch away, whether in a good or a bad sense, defend, deliver (self), escape, without fail, part, pluck, preserve, recover, rescue, rid, save, spoil, strip, surely, take (out).*

Just as God delivered the children of Israel, and me, He can and will deliver you from whatever has held you captive! I'm going to share four levels of deliverance that God had to take me through in order to go beyond. This list is not exhaustive to every area but are just some key areas that I believe every person will have to get free from if we are to access our good land.

Exodus 3:7-8

"And the LORD said, I have surely seen the affliction of my people which are in Egypt, and have heard their cry by reason of their taskmasters; for I know their sorrows; and I have come down to deliver them out of the hand of the Egyptians and to bring them up out of that land to a good and broad land, a land flowing with milk and

> *honey, to the place of the Canaanites, the Hittites, the Amorites, the Perizzites, the Hivites, and the Jebusites."*

Listen, don't ever believe that God has not seen or knows all of your afflictions, misery, all the times you have been mishandled and dealt with harshly. When you go through so much, you can tend to take hold of the thought that God doesn't care or why did He allow all this. Just know that God has just been waiting on you to cry out, to desire to be set free, healed and delivered. There are times when God will invade your space, but for the most part He is moved by your true and earnest plea for salvation. It's just like if you have children you become familiar with their cries and what they mean. See everything in the Kingdom is voice activated. It was their cry that got God's attention and it states that He came down to deliver them from out of the power of the Egyptians.

The children of Israel had to be delivered from Egypt, their environment, the place where they had been held captive for over 400 yrs.

LEVEL ONE: ENVIRONMENT

In deliverance many times the first thing God will do is remove you from the environment that has kept you from functioning at your maximum potential.

An environment is the surrounding or conditions in which a person lives or operates, territory, or domain. Environments represents small places and confinement. This is important because your environment effects four different areas, it affects how you

1. Live - your level of contentment in a surrounding or condition
2. Operate - how you do things
3. Activities - what you do
4. Learn - how you take in information

In other words, your environment effects your soul which is made up of three parts, your mind, will and emotions. Your soul will determine how you live, your behaviors, actions and your reasoning. Once you are out of the old environment God will begin to deal with your mind, wrong thinking, sight, and perception. Why? Because the Bible says that as a man thinks so is he. How you think, see, and perceive life has a great effect on how you live life.

Then there are emotions. God will deal with toxic emotions, how you feel about yourself and life. If we don't allow God to deal with our emotions, they will lead us into places God never designed. Or they will keep us in places that God has called us out of. Feelings of being emotionally attached will cause you to be connected to people and places that

God wants you to let go of and cause you to stay, even when you know it's not the best for you. As believers we are to be led by our Spirit, not our emotions.

Lastly, we need deliverance from our own will.

Will G2307- a determination, choice, inclinations, desire, pleasure, impulses, commands, precepts, to like and do something.

Let's look at a few things concerning our will.

1. Your will is where decisions are made, it is how we choose or not choose.
2. It governs our actions. (produces an action Godly or ungodly)
3. It communicates what we want.
4. It is where secret tendencies lie.
5. Our will is driven by lust, appetites, plans, passions, convictions, character, cravings, and longings that are usually fleshly or carnal (sensual).

Depending on how we were raised, many of us have illegal appetites. We desire things, people, and places that goes against God's desire and plan for our lives. We see that in the life of Jesus he said, "My meat is to do the will of Him that sent me." (John 4:34). What He was saying is that I've given my desires and appetites over to the will of my Father, and His passion and convictions kept Him in a place of submission to that will. Many of us struggle in this place.

This level has been extremely challenging for me as I always had a picture of what I wanted life to be and maybe you do to, but what you or I want doesn't always line up with what God wants. The one thing that I've found is that all my plans, dreams, and desires left me still hungry for more. I would accomplish one thing and immediately I was on to the next thing.

See, illegal appetites are driven by lust and according to James 4:2. It is our own lust that stirs up wars within. So many times, we think it's the devil but really, it's you yielding to your own lust instead of submitting to what God has and that creates much warfare. See it's like Paul who said when I would do good evil is always present (see Romans 7:21). The things I would do I don't do, and things I don't I find myself doing (see Romans 7:19).

It becomes intense when you find yourself continuing in patterns and behaviors that in your heart and soul you desire to be free of. Then in Romans 7:24 Paul goes on to ask this question, who will deliver me? When you are facing this kind of battle the only answer is deliverance, you need to be broken free from the spirit of bondage that conditions your soul to think, feel and desire things that God has not ordained for you.

This is so important because God has a purpose and a plan for your life. He brings you out of your environment to bring you into what He has prepared for you, so that He can place you in an environment that is conducive for your growth. A place that will nurture and cause you to flourish. Without deliverance you will spend your whole life barren, fruitless and empty.

PERSONAL NUGGET

Where I come from there was a saying, "You can take the person out the hood (Egypt) but you can't take the hood (Egypt) out of the person." This saying always bothered me because it suggests that no matter what I did, the things I learned in that environment would always govern my life. Let me tell you, how wrong that statement was. Getting out the "hood" (Egypt) was the best thing that happened to me because it was then that I was exposed to a different way of life. When I came out of that environment, I learned that my behavior could be changed, and I could change as well. Yes, it took some time to unlearn a lot of the wrong things I learned there but through deliverance the "hood" (Egypt) has been uprooted out of me!

LEVEL TWO: REBELLION

Exodus 6:9

"And Moses spake so unto the children of Israel: but they hearkened not unto Moses for anguish of spirit, and for cruel bondage."

Bondage creates rebellion. See when you feel as if you have been controlled, confined or limited in anyway, when you become free you can take on the mindset that no one will ever control you again!

You must be delivered from a rebellious spirit! Why, you may ask, because when we function in a rebellious spirit ultimately you are saying to God that I am displeased with your will for my life.

Rebellion is defined as to be contentious, be rebellious, be refractory, be disobedient towards, be rebellious against, defiance, bitter.

Here are some signs and symptoms that can help you to identify if you have or are operating in a rebellious spirit: *stubbornness, hardness of heart, witchcraft, mind control, slothfulness, stiff neck, procrastination, laziness, idolatry, deception, delayed obedience, partial obedience, fear, fear of failure, fear of success, fear of the unknown, lack of discipline , contention with God, argumentative, aggressiveness, hostile, touchy, defiant, difficult, resistant, inconsistent, inability to be flexible, inability to be affectionate, obstinacy , cynicism, ridicule, sarcasm, contempt, dogmatic, opinionated, perverse and having a problem with authority.*

The harsh treatment and undeserved hardship of the children of Israel caused them not to hearken to the voice of the Lord.

Hearken 8085 schema - To hear intelligently, pay attention, obedience, consent, consider, listen, understand, to obey, to proclaim, sound the alarm and respond to him.

When in rebellion, you will not listen to or respond to the Voice of God. That desire to do what you want to do will rise on the inside of you and cause your heart to become hardened to the voice of the Lord. That's what it means to have ears but not hear (see Jeremiah 5:21). You can know what God is asking of you and what He is saying to you, but because of rebellion you will not obey. This spirit can be so strong that even though like we discussed earlier, you may desire to obey but those manifestations will rise. Rebellion will cause you to always find a way around doing what God has for you and your soul will be justified in not doing it.

In the Bible there are many scriptures that provide answers to rebellion. I encourage you, after looking at the definition and manifestations of rebellion, to look up all the scriptures you can find on rebellion and seek Holy Spirit for the one that will bring deliverance to you. I will share with you the one that God has really impressed upon my heart and has helped me the most. I always knew that I didn't like to be told what to do. I wanted my way when it came to certain things. For some strange reason, I really didn't see it as a rebellious spirit until after an experience I had.

God was dealing with me and He spoke to me concerning the roots of rebellion. For me it was the absence of my father (you can study the effects of fatherlessness). There was a generational spirit that had been passed down in my bloodline. One morning I was in prayer and I was crying out to the Lord, asking Him many questions as I often times do when I'm trying to break free from something, He spoke these words to me "Receive My Grace." After that, immediately I was reminded of a scripture that I had previously looked at when doing a study on grace.

Hebrews 12:15 (ESV)

"See to it that no one fails to obtain (receive) the grace of God: that no root of bitterness springs up and causes trouble, and by it many become defiled:"

I want to look at several points in this scripture. Take a look at the phrase *fail to*. It means *to lack in excellence, worth, come to late, be inferior in power, influence and rank*. It means *to be left behind in the race and because of it fail to reach the goal*.

The word *grace* here is the Greek Key G5485 *charis*, meaning t*hat which affords joy, pleasure, delight, sweetness, charm, loveliness, good will, loving-kindness, favor. It refers to graciousness as gratifying, it is the divine influence upon the heart, and its reflection in life, including gratitude.* As I studied this scripture, that root of bitterness that we hold many times causes us to rebel against God. This is why it so important to receive God's grace or that which brings joy and pleasure, that which influences your heart and governs how you reflect on life.

Without God's grace, you will only focus on the negative, but His grace will cause you to have a different perception. You will no longer be bitter about what happened but when you really receive His grace, when you reflect on your life, joy will come because you will know that it was God's grace that brought you out of that situation. You then will become grateful and thankful that you aren't still there. Simply put GRATEFULNESS cancels REBELLION and BITTERNESS! When you can come to a place where you are grateful for what God has done for you, and what He has provided through His grace. You will want and desire to adhere to all He asks of you and His grace will provide you with the power to do so. With a grateful heart there is no way that God will leave you behind, you will reach the intended goal for your life!

PERSONAL NUGGET

Love creates desire, force creates rebellion!

When there is no bitterness in you, you will start believing that what God is asking, not requiring of you, is for your good. That type of love, God's love will always cause you to obey Him. John 14:15 states, that if we love Him, keep (obey) his commandments. Don't see God as something or someone who is holding you captive or forcing you to do anything. See Him as a Loving Father that is asking you to do what's best for you!

LEVEL THREE: SELF-PERCEPTION (GRASSHOPPER COMPLEX)

You must be delivered from wrong self-perceptions. Self-perception are your internal thoughts about yourself. It is the internal impression, arguments or reasons furnished by your own mind/heart, that dictates what you believe about yourself. This is important because what you think about yourself will establish the order of your life. Proverbs 4:23(b) says, *"...for out of it (your heart) are the issues of life."* Your internal thoughts will be communicated by your actions. In life you will have to actively pursue after what God has already given you, but your internal thoughts will dictate whether you obtain it or not.

The Bible says "*...as a man thinks in his heart, so is he.*" (see Proverbs 23:7). With a wrong self-perception, you will not run to what God has promised, but run from it!

Bondage has a way of making you think differently about yourself, your potential, and what you can and can't do!

Numbers 13:33 states that when the children of Israel saw giants, they thought they were grasshoppers in their own sight. Seeing the giants, that were bigger than them caused them to see themselves as being small. In their minds they thought surely, they were no match for them, there's no way we can defeat them.

The grasshopper complex will tell you that you lack knowledge, understanding, wisdom, and the skill to fulfill what God has already prepared for you.

Some other manifestations are insecurity, inferiority, self-doubt, self-imposed limitations, self-sabotaging, fear, fear of man, fear of what people think or will say about you, fear of failure, fear of success, fear of not being prepared or ready, and fear of not measuring up. It will cause you to be easily discouraged. Ask yourself this question, what lie or lies has the enemy told me about myself that has caused me to see myself differently than how God sees me?

One day, I had this dream. In the dream, there was a well-known Apostle and he asked me "What do you think is stopping you?" I responded that I had not been cared for or nurtured as a child. See, for me not being cared for gave me a wrong self-perception of myself. I didn't think I was valuable or worthy. I pondered on this dream for weeks. I remembered that someone once said that God doesn't ask you a question because He doesn't know the answer but because He wants to give you the answer.

So, one morning in worship God began to say to me that the answer I had given wasn't true. Wait, what do you mean it's not true, God? He then began to tell me that it wasn't that I wasn't nurtured that has stopped me, but it was the place of my desire to be nurtured that has stopped me. The truth was that because those desires to be cared for, had not been filled, it caused me to feed into the lie that the devil told me. I wasn't valuable, that I would always be less than. That is the furthest thing from the truth. I had allowed someone else's treatment of me to give me a false perception of myself. This is what was stopping me from moving forward.

Take some time and ask Holy Spirit to help you identify the lies that the enemy has fed you about yourself. As you identify them, you must replace it with the truth of God's Word about you and who you are. I can remember times when I would ask

God what He would want me to know, and He would say, *"You're loved."* He would say *"You're valuable "*, and most importantly, He would say *"You're enough!"*

So I speak those same words over you, and I encourage you to say what God says about you, not the lies of the enemy that says you're nothing, you're broken, God doesn't love you or why else would He have let that happen to you. Those are all lies of the enemy to stop you from seeing your true potential and the real power you hold within.

Your value doesn't come from without (external) but from within (internal). Your internal thoughts about you matter more than the thoughts and treatment of others!

How does God deal with your self-perception? He will oftentimes allow you to enter into situations that you are not prepared for, to teach you how to gain confidence in Him and yourself.

Proverbs 24:16 says, *"...A righteous man falls seven times, he rises again."*

You may fail, you may fall but you must rise again! Know that with every trial and with every situation, God is teaching you:

1. Persistence
2. How to build again

3. How to continue
4. What success is. Keep trying until you succeed

Remember this, every failure helps you to grow! Trials help you to really identify who you really are and what you're made of. The value that you hold, no matter what others think or what life has thrown at you! As you continue on you will then began to see the strength that you possess. You will discover the greatness that is within you and unless you hadn't gone through what you faced you wouldn't be able to see the GREATNESS that is you!

PERSONAL NUGGET

You don't need permission to be great. Give yourself permission to be GREAT!

Let me share with you where this came from. On a Sunday after church service, I had gone to the altar for prayer. I was in a season where I was battling with doing what God had called me to do because of self-image. As the Apostle prayed for me, out of her mouth came these words *"The Lords says, you don't need permission. If you are waiting on someone to give you permission, you'll be waiting, He also says give yourself permission to be great!"* Those words pierced my heart because I'm a strong person and to many I seemed very confident, but no one knew that I really struggled with a wrong self-perception, except God. I would like to say that I immediately took those words and ran with them, but I didn't. It took some time for me to become comfortable with who I am and what I possess down on the inside. Here's how I got there, and this is what you will need to do as well.

Encourage yourself, even if no one else believes in you, you must believe in yourself. Get free from wanting or needing someone else to tell you it's ok to BE YOU or to do what God called you to do.

Say this, *"I DON'T NEED ANYONE'S PERMISSION OR APPROVAL!"*

Make this declaration, I will allow myself to be great, no more self-sabotaging, no more self-imposed limitations, no more insecurities, I can and will be great, In Jesus Name, Amen!

LEVEL FOUR: YOUR PAST

You can be so focused on your past that you can't see what's right in front of you. The children of Israel's future were straight ahead of them, but because they were so traumatized by their past, they couldn't see the goodness that was before them. Their traumatic experience in Egypt caused them to not perceive and know God's goodness. So much so that they longed for what God had brought them out of. What would make a person want to return to bondage, 1 Corinthians 10:6 refers to it as lust, an unhealthy desire or an attachment for what had held them captive. It goes on to express that we are not to follow their example in 1 Corinthians 10:11.

These things happened to them as examples for us. They were written down to warn those who live at the end of the age. See your past is only significant if you allow it to be. Stop ruminating. You must choose to stop rolling over in your mind all the bad things that has happened to you. The enemy will have you rethinking over your past so that it will remove you from the present moment and flood you with negative emotions about it. The Bible says remember not the former things. Don't give too much attention to what happened to you, what you didn't have or get, but focus on your now and where God is taking you!

If you consider your past for too long, it can create a sense of jealousy and cause you to think that God isn't fair. You will begin to think that life isn't fair or else you would have gotten what someone else has. You have to know and believe that he has so much in store for you, you just have to receive it. Don't let anything rob you of your future.

Don't get stuck in your past, make a conscious decision to move forward. After all God didn't deliver you to stay stuck but he delivered you to show you things that you hadn't seen before, to do things you haven't done before, to experience things you haven't experienced before, and to take you places that you haven't gone before.

Make peace with your past cause it's just that! Don't ruminate on past regrets, past failures, past relationships, or past situations and circumstances that caused you shame. Let go of the shame, we've all endured or did things that we can't go back and undo, but you can move forward with a new perspective. You have to decide that you will not live in the chaos of your past! Many of our past wreaked havoc on us. But we have the ability to live a life filled with peace. There is peace after the storm!

Romans 6:4 says,

> "Therefore, we are buried with him by baptism into death: that like as Christ was raised up from the dead by the glory of the Father, even so we also should walk in newness of life."

There is a newness of life that In God we can experience! That means that in God your life can become fresh, new and exciting. He will give you a life beyond your wildest dreams or imaginations. If you would have told me way back then that I would be doing what I'm doing now I wouldn't have believed it, my life has been totally transformed by the power of God. He Is a God that takes what's dead and revives it, He takes what's broken and fixes it and He takes what brought you shame and turns it into honor and glory for His name's sake!

Just like He did with the children of Israel, God delivered them to go beyond the borders of bondage and He delivered them into purpose, with a promise of freedom! It is the same for you, you've been delivered with a purpose and promise so don't stay stuck or stagnate.

PERSONAL NUGGET

Giving birth to your future will make you forget your past! It is the Lord that impregnates you with purpose so that you forget all your toil and hardships in the previous seasons. When I went into labor with my daughter, I experienced pain that I had never felt, and to top it off I was in labor for close to three days. But, once I gave birth to her and saw her, I had forgotten all the pain I had just experienced. Giving birth cancelled out all the pain and it was well worth!

> Say this prayer, *"I am emancipated from what happened to me in my past. I decree that my family history no longer have influence over me. It's time to terminate any control that bondage has had over me in Jesus name, amen!"*

God has delivered us, but so many of us don't know or understand what happens after God brings us out of situations and circumstances. In the next chapter, you will be given the tools to understand why God delivered you and how to understand what God has for you next. You'll learn how to go beyond where you are now and access the purpose and promise God has for you!

POWER CONFESSIONS FOR DELIVERANCE

I decree that I am free from all bondage.

I decree that every bondage working against my future has been stripped of its power!

I decree that I will see the salvation of the Lord!

I decree that everything that has taken root from my old environment, be uprooted!

I decree that I will thrive and flourish in my new environment!

I decree the judgement, punishment and wrath of God be upon all my enemies!

I renounce and rebuke every spirit of rebellion, resentment, disobedience and hardness of heart!

I loose vexation upon every stubborn spirit that does not want to submit to God!

I decree that I will come into agreement with the will of God!

I decree that I will hearken to the voice of the Lord!

I decree that I receive the grace of God that breaks the powers of rebellion and bitterness!

I come out of agreement with any and all wrong self-perceptions!

I come out of agreement with every lie the enemy has told me!

I break the powers of insecurity, inferiority, self-doubt, and self-sabotaging spirits!

I decree that I am great, and I will do great things!

I decree that I am who I am by the grace and power of God!

I decree I am released from my past, and I remember the former things no more!

I decree from this point forward that my past has no hold on me!

I decree that old things are passed away and all things are made new!

I decree that my thinking, actions, behavior, and perceptions are new!

I decree that I receive the newness of life in Christ Jesus!

CHAPTER 3: BROUGHT OUT WITH A PURPOSE AND A PROMISE

You can't be satisfied with just coming out of Egypt, (bondage, slavery, captivity). You have to understand that God didn't bring you out to sit idle, to go along with the status quo, or to be satisfied with living an unfulfilled life, with nothing to look forward to. You have purpose and with that purpose there is a promise attached.

THE PURPOSE

Purpose is God's deliberate plan for you. In Luke 22:32 Jesus said to Peter "...*when you are converted go back and strengthen your brother.*" He also told him he would make him fishers of men. Peter's purpose had a promise connected to it. Jesus didn't say if you are converted, the promise was when you are converted. The word converted means to turn as in transition. In life you will go through many transition periods and places in order to get to the next place and fulfil your purpose.

The reason why He is delivering you is so that you can go back. Those same men that you used to fish with, labor with, work with, you must strengthen them. He wanted Peter to give them hope that this isn't all to their lives. Just getting up every day doing the same thing over and over but reveal to them that they have a purpose and a promise as well. The very system that you grew up in and then settled in your mind that you were getting away from, could very well be your purpose and promise!

Let's look at the life of Moses. Moses was raised in Pharaoh's house which gave him insight into the structure and systems of the Egyptians. Moses would then grow up, commit murder (Sidenote: God was giving him a burden for his people. He just handled it the wrong way and had to flee).

Moses saw the wickedness of Pharaoh and how the Egyptians treated the Israelites. Just like many of you, you grew up in injustice, maybe poverty, lack, or dysfunction and you didn't like it. It grieved you to see the conditions of your environment, the state of your family, the condition of your neighborhood, whatever it was, and you said to yourself, "I'm getting out of here." You began to believe that your circumstances would kill you, if you didn't get out. Pharaoh wanted to kill Moses.

Even bondage will kill you, if not physically, mentally and emotionally. So, at the time God will allow you to flee so that he can bring healing and wholeness to who you are. That's exactly what Moses did. He fled, but what he didn't know was that it was part of God's greater purpose and promise to a people. Yes, you are a part of God's greater purpose and promise to a people.

Exodus 2:23 says,

> "And it came to pass in process of time, that the king of Egypt died: and the children of Israel sighed by reason of the bondage, and they cried, and their cry came up unto God by reason of the bondage."

The phrase in the process of time gives us some insight. Process refers to a systematic series of actions directed to achieve results. Time refers to the period or the duration it will take to get you to the end result (purpose). God knows your end and He will create space (process) to get you to that end. Your time away from whatever you were delivered from gives you a chance to change and God to give you a different perspective of the things that happened to you there. The time Moses spent away from Egypt, gave God the opportunity to do the work in him that would be needed to then go back and fulfill his purpose there. Moses was God's response to the cry of the children of Israel as it goes on to say that those that were left in bondage began to cry out and their cry came before God.

Exodus 3:6-8 says,

> "Moreover, he said, I am the God of thy father, the God of Abraham, the God of Isaac, and the God of Jacob. And Moses hid his face; for he was afraid to look upon God.

And the LORD said, I have surely seen the affliction of my people which are in Egypt, and have heard their cry by reason of their taskmasters; for I know their sorrows;

And I am come down to deliver them out of the hand of the Egyptians, and to bring them up out of that land unto a good land and a large, unto a land flowing with milk and honey; unto the place of the Canaanites, and the Hittites, and the Amorites, and the Perizzites, and the Hivites, and the Jebusites."

These scriptures identify God's purpose and promise. God's purpose was to deliver them out of bondage. God's promise was to bring them into a good land, filled with provisions.

God didn't deliver you and bring you out of bondage just for you, but when you understand how God moves you know that He will often times use one person to free many. Let me encourage you: your life has purpose. God didn't allow you to go through everything you went through for nothing. You have to begin to perceive it through the heart and mind of God.

A basic definition for the word purpose is the very reason you exist. Take some time and think about the very things that has caused you the most pain and that is probably the very thing that God has called you too. God is a God, that will take the very thing that was meant for evil against you and turn for your good. One of my favorite scriptures in the Bible is connected to the story of Joseph, if you haven't read it go back and do so. (see Genesis 37-50).

Genesis 50:19-20

> *"And Joseph said unto them, Fear not: for am I in the place of God?*
>
> *But as for you, ye thought evil against me; but God meant it unto good, to bring to pass, as it is this day, to save much people alive."*

This particular scripture has kept me focused throughout the years when I wanted to give up. When the enemy wanted to remind me of all the anguish and trauma of my past, I used this scripture as a weapon and to remind myself that God has a purpose and promise connected to my pain.

Here are some key points from these verses:

1. The enemy will use anything and anybody even family to propagate evil against you.

2. Your response has to be that it is not the person, but the spirit of evil set up against my life that will want me to abort my purpose and promise.

3. God always has a plan

Genesis 37 started with a dream which revealed Joseph's purpose and promise and even when it looked like that purpose and promise was destroyed God was with him. Even in your hardest times always remember God's words are with you and everything he has planned for you shall surely come to pass.

Isaiah14:27 (MSG)

> "...this is the plan, plan for the whole earth, and this is the hand that will do it, reaching into every nation. God of angel armies has planted, who could ever cancel such plans? His is the hand that you reached out who can brush it aside?"

Listen, the only person or thing that can stop God's plan for you is YOU. The enemy can't stop you. My pastor says when things are happening, he often stops and yells out, "You can't stop me!" See, you have to remind yourself that the devil doesn't have that much power, but what he does is work deception to make you think you're powerless and that because of everything that has happened to you, you'll never reach purpose or your promise. You need to get like my pastor and declare today to whatever it is, "You can't stop me!"

You have a purpose just like Peter, Moses, Joseph! Your purpose will always benefit someone else. God didn't deliver you for just you. I remember once while in a church service, the presence and glory of God was so strong and as we continued in prayer, I had a vision. In this vision I could see that out of my womb there was a rope coming forth and at the end there was knots that led to other pieces of rope and so forth and so forth. I knew that it was God showing me the many lives that were connected to mine and how they would benefit from my deliverance.

God didn't anoint you just for you or the sake of being anointed. What God has placed on the inside of you will benefit the many lives that you are called to. Some examples of this principle we see in the bible are:

Peter- The Church
Moses – The children of Israel
Joseph – His family lineage
Jesus – The whole world

Don't let your purpose be perverted.

Exodus 3:12 says,

"And he said, Certainly I will be with thee; and this shall be a token unto thee, that I have sent thee: When thou hast brought forth the people out of Egypt, ye shall serve God upon this mountain."

They were delivered to serve God, but later on you see them beginning to worship idols. Also, with Moses the passion he had to see the Hebrews free was perverted and he went about it through murder.

The word *pervert* means *to use something outside its original design*. Moses was designed to be a deliverer not a murderer. Let's say you have a gift for entrepreneurship, and you were designed to make money, the enemy will pervert that into drug selling. You are by design using your gift to make money but how you are doing it has been perverted by the enemy. This is why the Bible says everything we do, do it as unto the Lord. Use your purpose for God, not for the devil.

A lot of times we never get the promise because we don't walk in purpose. Some of the children of Israel never saw the promise because they didn't understand their purpose.

You may be asking, *how can I access God's purpose for me*? Well the answer is through His mind. In God's mind is the instruction, information and deliberation you need. Here are some tools on how to access purpose.

Let's look at Jeremiah 23:18-(ESV),

> *"For who among them has stood in the council of the LORD to see and to hear his word, or who has paid attention to his word and listened?"*

1. *Stands in his presence.*

2. Hear his voice.

3. Pay attention to his words.

4. Truly listen, how you here affect how you obey.

5. Once you know what your purpose is you have a decision to make.

Once you discover your purpose, there is a very important question you must answer. The spiritual father over the church I belong to had asked this question in a conference he was teaching,

> *"Will you choose preference or purpose."-Apostle Stephen Garner*

There will always be something opposing your purpose trying to get you to abandon what God has for you. One of the greatest enemies of purpose is a broken focus. A broken focus will cause you to have your attention on your preferences, the things you want and desire instead of making the decision to put aside everything that takes you out of the will of God for your life.

God called you out with a purpose, so let me encourage you; Continue to press toward the mark of the high calling in Christ Jesus. I'll leave you with a few things to ponder about PURPOSE.

1. Purpose will take you outside your comfort zone.

2. Purpose will make you do things you've never done before.

3. Purpose requires humility.

4. Purpose requires sacrifice.

5. Purpose will get you up early and cause you to go to bed late.

6. Purpose will change your diet and environment.

7. Purpose will cause you to endure hardship.

8. Purpose will cause you to carve out your own path.

THE PROMISE

God's promise is His Word unto you, and you must value the promises of God.

Promise G1860 - an announcement, for information, pledge, especially a divine assurance of good, a message. (Made by God)

A promise is *the announcing of what God has spoken to you with his divine assurance to fill it.*

Acts 2:39

"For the promise is made unto you, and to your children, and to all that are afar off, even as many as the Lord our God shall call."

Those that are called to God, have a promise. There are promises that are for all because God is not a respecter of person. Then there are promises that are uniquely made and spoken over your life.

2 Peter 1:4

"Whereby are given unto us exceeding great and precious promises: that by these ye might be partakers of the divine nature, having escaped the corruption that is in the world through lust."

We all have precious promises that God has given to us. Here are a few promises that applies to us all:

SALVATION/FORGIVENESS OF SINS

Isaiah 53:10

"Yet it pleased the LORD to bruise him; he hath put him to grief: when thou shalt make his soul an offering for sin, he shall see his seed, he shall prolong his days, and the pleasure of the LORD shall prosper in his hand."

SONSHIP

Romans 9:4

"Who are Israelites; to whom pertaineth the adoption, and the glory, and the covenants, and the giving of the law, and the service of God, and the promises;"

HOLY SPIRIT

John 14:26

"But the Comforter, which is the Holy Ghost, whom the Father will send in my name, he shall teach you all things, and bring all things to your remembrance, whatsoever I have said unto you."

BLESSINGS

Galatians 3:14

"That the blessing of Abraham might come on the Gentiles through Jesus Christ; that we might receive the promise of the Spirit through faith."

RIGHTEOUSNESS

Romans 4:11

"And he received the sign of circumcision, a seal of the righteousness of the faith which he had yet being uncircumcised: that he might be the father of all them that believe, though they be not circumcised; that righteousness might be imputed unto them also:"

WEALTH AND PROSPERITY

Deuteronomy 8:18

"But thou shalt remember the LORD thy God: for it is he that giveth thee power to get wealth, that he may establish his covenant which he sware unto thy fathers, as it is this day."

HEALING

1 Peter 2:24

> *"Who his own self bare our sins in his own body on the tree, that we, being dead to sins, should live unto righteousness: by whose stripes ye were healed."*

Then there are specific messages that God decrees over your life through prophetic utterances spoken through God's chosen vessels that, with your participation, will come to pass. With your specific promises there could be conditions attached to them. Meaning they will only come to pass if you follow the instruction given. See the children of Israel didn't receive their promise for multiple reasons and they spent years wandering in the wilderness instead of accessing the land that was promised to them.

A lot of times when you first come out of bondage, it looks like nothing is happening. It can appear that you are encountering the same things, situations, and circumstances over and over. Just like the children of Israel who went around the same mountain for 40 years. Even though it doesn't appear that anything is happening it is.

The wilderness is where God test and tries your heart, and whatever he can't use, will be exposed. God will allow you to experience certain things over and over to show you what's in your heart.

Not only does the wilderness expose your heart but it also gives you an opportunity to learn the ways of God.

Your wilderness season is necessary, and here are a few more reasons why.

1. It is an opportunity to deal with the holes in your foundation.
2. It sanctifies and cleanses you.
3. It is where God begins to rid you of your past.
4. It is your training on how to deal with problems and issues that you face.
5. It is in the wilderness that trust in God is built.

Everything you learn in the wilderness, if you submit and yield to it, will prepare you to access your promise. You can't enter a new place with an old mentality. The wilderness will work Egypt out of you. Everything you picked up while in bondage will be challenged in the wilderness so that you can learn a new way of doing things in your promise land.

You may be asking well how do I get my promise?

Hebrews 6:12 says,

> *"That ye be not slothful, but followers of them who through faith and patience inherit the promises."*

This scripture gives us some keys that will help you obtain what God has promised you.

1. *Keep at it until you finish. You must have the ability to finish what you started which will require you to work hard.*

2. *Don't drag your feet- you can't be slothful or slow moving when it comes to your promise.*

3. *Stay the course- you must be committed not just to the promise, but to the process as well.*

4. *Look to those that have gone before you-it will encourage you when you want to quit.*

5. *You must believe:*

- *God's authority and power.*
- *God's Word. He cannot lie.*
- *God doesn't change his mind or plan, no matter what it looks like.*
- *God is not unjust or unfair.*
- *God is able.*
- *God is faithful.*
- *God desires to bless you.*

6. *Receive – this implies that there has to be a response on your part. You must pursue and take possession of what God has already given you.*

7. *You must have faith for the promise. Say this, Lord give me faith for the Promise!*

My Apostle teaches that faith is not about how much faith you have, but instead how long you can maintain your faith. So, when you look at little faith it translates to short sustained faith. Sustain means to keep up or keep going, as an action or process.

So, for many it's a place where God wants to see as well as the devil how long can you go under pressure. God and the enemy will test your adversity quotient.

The Bible says in Galatians 6:9,

> "Be not weary in well doing for if you faint not you will reap a harvest or get to the promise in due time."

The question becomes how long you can endure without giving way or yielding to the enemy that wants you to quit. Satan wants to see if he can wear you out; if he can get you to sin or breakdown under the pressure, through the tactic of physical or mental exhaustion. Have you ever found yourself saying things like "I'm just tired, I'm tired of fighting, I'm tired of waiting?' Or you find yourself always being irritated by something or someone. Irritation is another tactic of the enemy to create interruptions. Irritants stops progression, and the enemy knows that if he can't get you to stop and quit, he will settle for delaying your process, because it is easier to maintain momentum, then to have to get it back. So, no matter what, keep moving.

From God's perspective what is your capacity to carry the weight of his purpose and promise? God is looking at your ability to not slip or breakdown under whatever pressure that comes.

Matthew 14:29-30 says,

> *"And he said, Come. And when Peter was come down out of the ship, he walked on the water, to go to Jesus. But when he saw the wind boisterous, he was afraid; and beginning to sink, he cried, saying, Lord, save me."*

During the process to get to your promise, there will be distractions, hardships, sufferings, winds and the question you must ask yourself is, "What will cause me to waiver?" Will it be the winds, will it be sickness, will lack of finances, what will cause you to lose your faith? Take a moment and search and be truthful with yourself, because only when you expose it then you can fight against it and know how to strengthen your faith in that area.

Whatever you find, deal with it and strive to get to the place that the answer is nothing will make you waiver, because that's what commitment is. Ask yourself, *am I committed to the process and promise?*

Ask yourself *am I willing to wait for the promise no matter how long it takes?*

If you answered "no" to either of these questions, it is an indication that you have some enemies fighting against your promise.

ENEMIES OF PROMISE

Some of the enemies of promise are doubt, unbelief, lack of commitment, impatience, murmuring, complaining and fear.

Here are a few more enemies of promise:

SLOTHFULNESS/PROCRASTINATION

Don't allow your heart to grow dull, or lose your enthusiasm

UNCLEANNESS, SIN AND IDOLATRY

WORKS OF THE FLESH

Impatience will cause you to walk in the flesh. Make sure you don't try to make the promise happen by coming up with your own plan through the works of the flesh.

You must drive them out and utterly destroy them. We will talk about some warfare tactics in a later chapter.

Out of all the children of Israel there were only two that went into the promise land, Joshua and Caleb. They withstood the wilderness and because of it, they accessed what God had spoken over them forty years prior. Throughout the forty years, they didn't waiver, they trusted God and stayed committed to the process. Let their story be an encouragement that no matter the situation or how long it takes, the promise is possible!

POWER PRAYER

Father, I thank You that You have brought me out with a purpose and promise. I don't take it lightly or for granted the assignment You have for me! I thank You for your deliberate plan that You have for me. So today I make a decision to do everything in my power to come into alignment with and fulfill all that You have called me to.

I renounce and come out of agreement with everything that would oppose my destiny. I renounce and break every power of doubt, unbelief, wavering, double-mindedness, fear of failure, fear of success, lack of commitment, slothfulness, procrastination, laziness, delay, impatience, preferences, everything that wants to pervert my purpose, frustrations, aggravations, and disappointments, in the name of Jesus!

POWER CONFESSIONS FOR PURPOSE AND PROMISE

I decree that I was created for the purposes of God!

I decree that nothing shall stop the assignment, purpose and promise that God has ordained for me!

I decree I am a person of purpose!

I decree that I respond to the purpose of God for my life! I decree that I will maximize my potential!

I decree that I will not settle for mediocracy, I am exceptional and extraordinary!

I decree that I am committed, dedicated and determined to fulfill every purpose of God!

I decree that I will be intentional about my purpose and promise!

I decree that I have passion, patience and power to fulfill every purpose and promise!

I decree that I will not abort my purpose and promise!

I decree that I will stay in the process until the end!

I decree that I will follow through, execute and complete every assignment!

I decree that I will be willing to come out of my comfort zone in order to access purpose & the promise!

I decree that every promise shall become my reality!

I decree that I believe every word God has spoken over my life!

I decree that the promises of God are Yes and Amen!

CHAPTER 4: IT'S POSSIBLE

Bondage and confinement are designed to make you think that whatever you were born or purposed to do is impossible. Luke 18:2 says, *"And he said, the things which are impossible with men are possible with God."*

The word *impossible,* Greek Key G102 means *without strength, impotent, powerless, weakly, disable, unable to be done, could not do.*

The truth is, in our own strength it is impossible, but with God it's possible and deliverance allows us to be able to think, feel and see that it is. Many times, we try to fulfill a God-given promise without experiencing freedom, and without Him. The best thing we can do is depend on the giver of the promise. He never gives a promise without provision! The reality of living your life in God is this, the things that you could not do, once your connected to Him now you can. It's the ability to do things that don't make sense to man or your mind because of your background, your environment, your upbringing, your lack of skill and knowledge. You must become that person that believes God for what looks impossible.

To get a better understanding we will pull from the life of David and the children of Israel and how they determined what was possible or impossible. It didn't look like the children of Israel could defeat the giants in the land. When we are connected to God and because He is Almighty it becomes possible to defeat any giant. David proves this in 1 Samuel 17. There was no way that this little boy, shepherd boy was able to defeat this giant, but David knew the secret. He didn't trust in his own strength. He depended on God.

Let's go a little deeper, because everything starts with God. If you break the word down impossible, the suffix and prefix consist of two words.

Im- means without God

Possible - G145- Able, powerful, might, strong, mighty in wealth and influence; strong in soul, to bear calamities and trials with fortitude and patience; strong in Christian virtue, to be able to do something, having power for something, and excellency in something.

As we look at that definition, one of the things David referred to was that he had been trained for war, to fight things bigger than him. He became excellent at destroying things. He said he had defeated a lion and bear (see 1 Samuel 17:34-35) before, so when he looked at Goliath, he was not afraid, and on the contrary, he knew it was possible to defeat him.

On the other hand, the children of Israel had been in bonds so long they didn't even think that they could fight. Which is why in Judges 3:2, tells of how

God took them the long way to teach them how to fight. The children of Israel weren't excellent at war, but God put them in a position to be able to develop that skill and become excellent at it.

For so many of us we want to know why this and why that but let me tell you if you've gone through anything it is to show you the strength that is in you and that's how you learn to fight.

David wouldn't have been as confident in his ability to defeat Goliath if he hadn't already had to defeat the lion and the bear. Can I tell you that what you're facing before you is nothing, why, because you've already faced some things that you thought would kill you but it didn't? So now take the skills and strategies and SLAY every giant that stands before you.

If we look at the definition of possible again it said *strong in soul and the ability to bear calamities and trials with fortitude and patience.* This was the children of Israel problem and it is many of ours today. They were weak in soul instead of strong in soul.

You might be asking yourself, *"How do I know if I'm weak in my soul?"* One indication is that you *faint at the very sight of trouble.* According to Proverbs 24:10 *if you faint in the day of adversity your strength is small.* To faint means to forsake, be slothful, withdraw and be weak or weakened. Fainting starts in your soul.

Soul is the Hebrew Key H5315 *nephesh* and Greek Key G5590 *psyche* which refers to *your mind, will, and emotions*. As we dissect what it means to be weak in soul, I'll give you an example for each part of your soul.

Your mind deals with your reasoning, thinking and how you process information. Here is an example: Your mind says, "*I don't know how I'm going to do this, or even think that I can do this.*" You are being driven by negative patterns of thinking which then create negative emotions.

Your emotions are what you feel and your reaction to that feeling. Example: Your emotions says, "*I don't feel like I have the strength to do _____.*" You are being driven by negative emotions which creates negative action.

Your will deals with the ability to choose or decide. Example: Your will says, "*I don't even have the desire to do this.*" This will cause you to become paralyzed and you will never go any further than where you are.

God will tell you to do something, but the condition of your soul will determine whether or not it's possible. The state of your soul determines the outcome of your life.

Ask yourself, "Is my soul strong or weak"

We're going to look at one of the most prevalent places in the Bible that gives the best depiction of this, the life of Jesus when he was in the Garden of Gethsemane. We're going to pull from the gospel's depiction of the same account. As we start with Luke's account, you will see how the state of the souls of Jesus and his disciples dictated how they would handle the challenge that was before them.

Luke 22:39-41 says,

> *"And he came out, and went, as he was wont, to the mount of Olives; and his disciples also followed him.*
>
> *And when he was at the place, he said unto them, Pray that ye enter not into temptation.*
>
> *And he was withdrawn from them about a stone's cast, and kneeled down, and prayed, Saying, Father, if thou be willing, remove this cup from me: nevertheless, not my will, but thine, be done.*
>
> *And when He arose from Prayer, and was come to His disciples, He found them sleeping for sorrow."*

The disciples had allowed their mind, will, and emotions to get the best of them. How do we know this? Let's look at Matthew chapter 16, these are the words Peter spoke to Jesus after He told them the things which was to come concerning His crucifixion.

Matthew 16:22

"Then Peter took him, and began to rebuke him, saying, Be it far from thee, Lord: this shall not be unto thee."

Mark 14:40

"And when he returned, he found them asleep again, (for their eyes were heavy,) neither wist they what to answer him."

From examining these scriptures, we can conclude that the state of the disciple's souls was weak.

THE MIND

Peter didn't process correctly the information that Jesus gave him therefore his thoughts about it led him to rebuke Jesus.

THE EMOTIONS

The sorrow that they were experiencing did not produce the right response to Jesus request.

THE WILL

In the most trying time of their leaders' life, they decided to go to sleep instead of doing what He asked them to do.

The state of the disciple's soul ultimately caused them to fail at what was asked of them, Jesus told them to pray. They had the ability to pray. Matthew

6:9 (NIV) says, *"This, then is how you should pray:"* Jesus then goes on to teach them how to pray. So it wasn't that they didn't know or couldn't pray but the state of their soul made it impossible for them to pray."

Jesus on the other hand knew that the only way He could do what was before him, was to tap into the source of strength needed that would make him able to do it, what did He do? He prayed!

This is so important because when we're faced with challenging things, the Bible says in Exodus 15:9, *"He pursues, then overtake, devise and destroys all in the place of our soul. The enemy pursues access into your soul through vexation, bitterness, wounds, grief, affliction, and persecution."*

One of the most important ways we strengthen our souls is through that place of PRAYER. Prayer strengthens your soul this is the pattern that Jesus gives.

It wasn't that Jesus didn't face the same things you and I go through, but the difference is he did what most of us don't do, he strengthened his soul. He had to deal with every aspect of his soul. Matthew 26:36 through 38 states Jesus soul *was sorrowful even unto death.* Often times your soul is what kills what God has ordained and promised for you. Have you ever had an idea or something creative you wanted to do and immediately your mind said that's impossible, and then you didn't pursue after that thing? It was dead before it even started. The great thing about our God is he is the Resurrection (see John 11:25) and specializes in reviving dead things.

If we look a little closer to the scriptures three times, we see Jesus dealing with every aspect of his soul.

In Matthew 26:39 He states,

"And he went a little further, and fell on his face, and prayed, saying, O my Father, if it be possible, let this cup pass from me: nevertheless, not as I will, but as thou wilt." The focus here is "if it is possible".

In His MIND, He was trying to figure out another way to solve the problem, his mind is trying to convince him or confuse him about what God has said. Questioning brings confusion.

In Matthew 26:42 (NIV) He says,

"Unless I drink it".

His WILL is refuting the plan of God and at that moment He had a decision to make, whether He was going to listen to His emotions or not.

In Luke 22:44 it says He prayed the same words and that He was in agony.

In His EMOTIONS, there was a severe struggle and wrestling taking place. He was in a struggle for a victory.

We must do as Jesus did, and contend in that place of prayer until we bring our mind, will, and emotions under the subjection of the will of the Father! Based on these scriptures we looked at some signs of a weak soul are questioning, confusion, rebellion, you want to disconnect, yield to slothfulness, tiredness, you don't deal with adversity well, and distress.

Some signs of a strong soul are:

>*Patience- Hebrews 6:12, Hebrews 12:1*
>*Stability- Colossians 2:7*
>*Endurance – Hebrews 6:15*
>*The ability to wait on God- Psalm 37:34*

Another reason the state of your soul is so important is in your soul is the power of knowing, desiring, deciding and acting. Now ask yourself where do you fall? Be honest because the Bible teaches that we are to examine ourselves. If you have discovered that your soul is weak that's OK, follow the pattern of Jesus and pray! Prayer not only strengthens our soul, but it activates the Spirit of God within you.

The Bible says the spirit is willing, but the flesh is weak. When you activate your spirit, it gives you the power of God, the power of knowing, desiring, deciding, and acting on what God has said. The spirit is always willing to accomplish the work of the father. So even when your mind, will and emotions says no, your spirit will say YES! Willingness is a readiness through Holy Spirit that makes you available to the passion, power, and patience that's needed.

There are three things we need in order to carry out purpose and promise:

PASSION

Passion dictates your willingness; You can't do what you are not passionate about. Passion also causes you to sacrifice and it gives you the ability to lay your life down.

Acts 1:3 says,

> "To whom also he shewed himself alive after his passion by many infallible proofs, being seen of them forty days, and speaking of the things pertaining to the kingdom of God:""

PATIENCE

Patience helps you to wait for God's timing not move in your own timing.

Romans 8:25 says,

"But if we hope for that we see not, then do we with patience wait for it.""

POWER

Power is the fortitude to carry out the assignment.

Acts 1:8 says,

"But ye shall receive power, after that the Holy Ghost is come upon you:"

PRAYER. Prayer is what helps us come into agreement with God's plan.

In Luke 22:42, we find Jesus saying nevertheless not my will, but your will be done.

The devil will fight you in the place of agreement because he knows that you won't see what God has said until you come into agreement with what God has said. The devil also knows that the will of God for your life is far more superior, it is greater, His will is more excellent, and it far surpasses anything you could ever plan or desire for yourself!

Jesus prayed until He became one with the Father's mind, will, and emotion. Many times, we don't come into agreement with what God has chosen because sometimes God's way will bring pain. Prayer helps with what the flesh does not or cannot do.

When dealing with the impossible, prayer:

BRINGS UNDERSTANDING

Colossians 1:9 says,

> "For this cause we also, since the day we heard it, do not cease to pray for you, and to desire that ye might be filled with the knowledge of his will in all wisdom and spiritual understanding;" '

GIVES US THE ABILITY TO DO GREAT AND GLORIOUS THINGS.

James 5:16 says,

> "Confess your faults one to another, and pray one for another, that ye may be healed. The effectual fervent prayer of a righteous man availeth much.""

RESTRAINS CORRUPT DESIRES. (WE PRAY UNTIL THOSE URGES PASSES.)

Matthew 6:13 says,

> "And lead us not into temptation but deliver us from evil: For thine is the kingdom, and the power, and the glory, forever. Amen.""

HELPS US BEAR TRIALS AND TROUBLES.

Romans 8:26 says,

> "Likewise, the Spirit also helpeth our infirmities: for we know not what we should pray for as we ought: but the

> *Spirit itself maketh intercession for us with groanings which cannot be uttered.""*

If you have not read the complete account of Jesus in the Garden of Gethsemane please go back and read it for yourself. We take a lot of the key components from this one story because at the end of it is that Jesus, through prayer, fulfilled his assignment in the earth. It allowed him to go to the cross on behalf of our sins, that we may experience deliverance, freedom, and wholeness.

POWER PRAYER

> *Father, in the name of Jesus I confess my faults to You and I seek your help, and strength to be able to do what You've called me to do. Father break the powers of confusion, distress, rebellion, doubt, unbelief, and laziness that has tried to keep me stuck. I ask that You strengthen my soul that I have passion, patience, power, and stability in my soul and the ability to endure everything that comes my way. I decree I will follow the pattern that Jesus set before me and I will pray earnestly without ceasing. Father You said that what was impossible in my own strength is possible with You, so I press into You believing that all things are possible in Jesus name, Amen.*

When I received this revelation of what's possible with God the Holy Spirit instructed me for a period of 7 days to believe God for something that seemed impossible for me to achieve outside of Him. Why

7, because 7 is the number of completion and perfection. I want to do the same for you, for the next 7 days I want you to write out something that seems impossible. This exercise will do 1 of 2 things or both, it will expand your capacity to believe for bigger and better, or it will reveal your low level of expectation. If you find that you don't have 7 things to believe for ask Holy Spirit to place in your heart dreams that exceed your expectation.

I'll give you an example, this comes straight from my journal entry

Today I'm believing you God for the ability to build a multi-million-dollar center that is a safe place for people to come to get all kinds of resources. This center will offer emotional counseling, health education, recreation, gym, senior services, financial education and services, and recovery support. It's possible with God!

I must admit probably by day 4 or 5, I was struggling, but I prayed, and I completed it. Every now and again I go back to those entries and read them and declare them because faith comes by hearing! I will say that now today those dreams have become more possible in my heart than when I first wrote them.

Day 1
Today I'm believing God for _____ It's Possible with God!

Day 2
Today I'm believing God for _____ It's Possible with God!

Day 3
Today I'm believing God for _____ It's Possible with God!

Day 4
Today I'm believing God for _____ It's Possible with God!

Day 5
Today I'm believing God for _____ It's Possible with God!

Day 6
Today I'm believing God for _____ It's Possible with God!

Day 7
Today I'm believing God for _____ It's Possible with God!

POWER CONFESSIONS FOR THE SOUL

My soul is not weak My soul is not broken

My soul is not sorrowful My soul is not in anguish My soul is not divided My soul is whole

My soul is not slothful or idle My soul is restored- Psalms 23:3

My soul is refreshed- Proverbs 25:13

My soul is healthy and healed- Psalm 41:4

My soul is delivered from the pit- Job 33:30

My soul is alive- Genesis 12:13

My soul will bless the Lord- Psalms 103:2

My soul is purified- 1Peter 1:22

My soul is not discouraged- Numbers 21:4

My soul is diligent- Deuteronomy 4:9

My soul seeks and loves the Lord- Deuteronomy 6:5

My soul is not bitter- 1 Samuel 1:10

My soul is redeemed out of all adversity- 2 Samuel 4:9

My soul is not weary- Jeremiah 31:2

My soul waits for the Lord- Psalms 33:20

My soul is humbled through fasting- Psalms 35:13

My soul has been rescued from destruction- Psalms 35:17

My soul is at peace- Psalms 55:18

My soul is satisfied- Psalms 63:5

My soul follows hard after the Lord- Psalms 63:8

My soul is strong- Psalms 138:3

My soul knows right well- Psalms 139:4

My soul is out of prison- Psalms 142:7

My soul is filled with knowledge- Proverbs 2:10

My soul magnifies the Lord- Luke 1:46

My soul is anchored in Jesus- Hebrews 6:19

My soul is at rest- Matthew 11:29

I break every unhealthy soul tie

I surrender my soul to the word of God- Psalms 19:7

The word of the Lord is in my soul- Deuteronomy 11:18

I will not despise my own soul- Proverbs 15:32

CHAPTER 5: I'M GOING IN

Before I entered into this new decade, God began to tell me to make this declaration, *I'm going into my Good Land!* What does that mean you might ask? Well, our good land is where our purpose and promise will be fulfilled. I realized that God told me to declare this because our words carry weight, the more you declare a thing faith will arise. Romans 10:17 declares, *"So then faith cometh by hearing, and hearing by the word of God."* The more you hear a word it ignites faith in you to believe that the word of the Lord can and will come to pass. As faith ignites and increase you then come into agreement with that word.

This is so important because Amos 3:3 says *"How can two walk together unless they be agreed."* This means that there needs to be agreement. Yes, God needs your agreement! God will not force you to do anything, He simply presents you with His will and you have to choose whether or not you're going to come into alignment with it or not! The word walk here is go, move and journey, in other words come into divine alignment with the path He has chosen for you. In order to go into the good land God has set for you, first you have to come together, be united and become one with Him on this journey. As you become one then there will be agreement.

This word *agreed* is the Hebrew Key H3259 and means *to fix upon by agreement, to direct in a certain position, to engage and to be set.* As you fix your heart towards the promise you will find yourself going into the direction that God has designated for you which will cause you to be rightly Positioned for the Promise!

When in agreement it will cause you to be obedient to the way God will have you to go to get to your good land. See without obedience we often times try to get to what God has for us outside of the way he has designed for us. We will try to make it happen in our own timing and strength; I know all about this to well. For many years I tried to do it my way but realized that only got me back to square one. I had to realize that if I was going to go into my good land it would require my complete obedience to God.

Exodus 24:7 says,

> *"And he took the book of the covenant and read in the audience of the people: and they said, All that the LORD hath said will we do, and be obedient."*

You too must realize that if you are going to enter the place God has ordained for you it requires obedience (compliance, submission to counsel, observing, requirements, attentive, hearkening, conform my conduct) to God's command. The biggest problem many in the bible had not just the children of Israel was they did not obey God's word. The Word of God is filled with scriptures concerning obedience. As a matter of fact, it tells us specifically to obey His voice.

As we discussed earlier, God's promise is His announcement to you and what He has spoken and proclaimed over you. You must have an ear to hear, meaning you must hear with the intent to do all of what you heard. If you look at the life of Moses in Numbers 20, one act of disobedience caused Him to forfeit his promise and denied him access into the good land. Numbers 20:11 says, *"Then Moses lifted up his hand and struck the rock twice with his rod."* In Numbers 20:8 God told him to speak to the rock. He failed to follow the instruction of the Lord. The bible tells us if we are willing and obedient, we will eat the good of the land (Isaiah 1:19). You and I must learn obedience and that is even in our suffering. Jesus learned obedience by the things He suffered. He was in agony, sweating droplets of blood but yet He choose to obey rather than to disobey God.

He knew what was at stake the souls of the world were on the line. Remember we talked about it's not just for you but those that you are called to.

Romans 5:19

"For as by one man's disobedience many were made sinners, so by the obedience of one shall many be made righteous."

If you fail to obey God not just your promise and access to the good land is on the line but all those that are connected to you. Someone else promise is locked on the inside of you. Your disobedience as well as your obedience will affect the lives of many that's why you must obey God

The thing with obedience is it will require you to be Bold! Look at the life of Joshua. God told him in Joshua chapter 1, multiple times that he only should be strong and courageous. The word courageous in the passage translate to bold. It will require boldness on your part to go where God is taking you. Bold means to go beyond the usual limits of conventional thought in action. To be imaginative, not hesitate to break the rules of propriety (not God's rules), and to not hesitate or be fearful in the face of actual or possible rebuff or danger. Going into your next may be totally outside of your normal and will cause you at times to be fearful. Why because most of the time whatever God has called you to, is going to be greater than you. It will cause you to question everything about yourself. You will find yourself wanting to make excuses like, I don't have the resources or capacity to do what God has called me to, I'm not smart enough. This one is my favorite, I don't even know how to begin doing what God has said, I made that excuse for years. Most of the things God called me to do, I didn't have a clue and in and of myself there was no way I could possibly get it done. After I strengthened my soul, I found that there were some more steps that I had to take and I am going to share with you how I have gone beyond my limitations, above the things I could think or imagine.

1. *YOU MUST ELIMINATE EXCUSES.*

Moses made excuse but his excuses kindled the anger of God, let's look at Exodus 4:1, then 10-17.

Exodus 4:1 says,

"And Moses answered and said, But, behold, they will not believe me, nor hearken unto my voice: for they will say, The LORD hath not appeared unto thee"

Excuse #1- *They won't believe me, nor hearken to my voice.*

What he really was saying is, who am I that people will believe that you called me to do this. So many times, we allow what others think or believe about us stop us. Let's just be clear there will always be naysayers that will not believe God has called you! They will want to hold you to your past and who you used to be see Moses was a Murderer prior to this and he probably thought to himself that's why the people wouldn't believe that God choose him. The bible says that God chooses the weak and the foolish things to confound the wise. So yes, no matter what you have done, know that God can and will use you!

Exodus 4:10-12 says

"And Moses said unto the LORD, O my Lord, I am not eloquent, neither heretofore, nor since thou hast spoken unto thy servant: but I am slow of speech, and of a slow tongue.

And the LORD said unto him, Who hath made man's mouth? or who maketh the dumb, or deaf, or the seeing, or the blind? have not I the LORD?

Now therefore go, and I will be with thy mouth, and teach thee what thou shalt say."

Excuse #2- *I am not eloquent, slow of speech, and slow of tongue.*

He began to point out to God all of what he (Moses) himself seen as flaws. Listen, God is not bothered by your flaws, He made you! The Bible says God knows the number of hairs on your head, so surely your flaws are not a surprise to God. In fact, it assures Him of your dependence on Him. In verse

12 He said, *"I will be your mouth and I will teach you what to say and how to speak"*. God will provide you with whatever you need!

Exodus 4:13-15 (ESV) says,

"But he said, "Oh, my Lord, please send someone else."

Then the anger of the LORD was kindled against Moses and he said, "Is there not Aaron, your brother, the Levite? I know that he can speak well. Behold, he is coming out to meet you, and when he sees you, he will be glad in his heart.

You shall speak to him and put the words in his mouth, and I will be with your mouth and with his mouth and will teach you both what to do."

Excuse #3- *Please send someone else.*

He was saying please send anybody but me or why me and sometimes you may feel the same way. You might be saying Lord I know there is someone else more qualified, more skilled, or just all around more suitable so why me? Let me ask you this question that I had to ask myself, WHY NOT YOU? Sometimes we can get so focus on why we shouldn't and never ponder why we should. If not you than who else will? I believe God choose Moses specifically because of what he knew about the Egyptian system. He grew up there. Yes, God could have sent someone else, but He didn't want to, He had chosen Moses for that assignment before he was placed in his mother's womb. You have been handpicked and chosen by God specifically to do what He has called you to do. God wants YOU!

When I look back on every excuse, it gave me permission to stay stuck in my dysfunction. It facilitated me being disobedient to what God desired for me. This may be the case for you too, but I say eliminate those excuses. They don't have validity and they are of no importance. Listen there is nothing more important than you entering the place God has for you.

2. YOU MUST DEAL WITH YOUR FEARS.

One of the biggest problems the children of Israel had were they were afraid of the giants in the land. They let their fears cause them to withdraw and retreat instead of advancing into the place God had set for them. Fear has an assignment and it is to make you run away or at very best be hesitant about what God told you to do. The voice of Satan comes to bring fear, but God's voice brings faith. If the devil can't stop, you he will settle for delaying the process. As we talked about earlier the longer it takes the more likely you will faint and forfeit your promise. This is why we must be bold enough to do whatever it is anyway. The bible says in 2 Tim 1:7 that God hasn't given us a spirit of fear, but power love and a sound mind. When you are afraid you must begin to declare the word of the Lord because faith filled words cancel fear filled thoughts in your mind. You must tap into the Love of the Father because His perfect loves cast out all fear (see 1 John 4:18). You have to believe in the divine power that is in you that will cause you tread over all the power of the enemy and know there is nothing that can hurt you (see Luke 10:19).

Simply put, you must face your giants because if you don't you will either return back to bondage or stay wandering around the wilderness. Giants represent that which intimidates you. What God has for you will always be bigger than you. You must approach it the way Caleb and Joshua did not the children of Israel. In Numbers 13:30, Joshua and Caleb stilled the people before Moses and said, let us go up at once and possess it; for we are well able to overcome it. You have to first still yourself, command all fears and intimidation to be silent! Secondly, you must go, take action, run to the battle not from the battle. Lastly, you must know the ability that God has given you!

Knowing your ability means you will have to understand how to establish your dominion over your enemy.

Genesis 1:26 declares that we have authority and we must exercise that authority, which is our legal right according to Psalm 149:9,

> "To execute upon them the judgment written: this honour have all his saints. Praise ye the LORD."

Part of that authority means that you and I can carry out and enforce the judgements of God against the adversary. This is important because the term adversary implies that there is going to be warfare. You have to know that even though God has already given you the promises, you have an adversary that wants to oppose God's will for your life in any way that he can. This is why we must develop spiritual stamina in the place of warfare. The bible uses a lot of military language, it tells us we must be good soldiers (see 2 Timothy 2:3). So, in order to fight against the adversary, we must become warriors.

A warrior is *one that will engage or is experienced in warfare, he shows great vigor, courage or aggressiveness when in battle, he defeats his competitors and he will engage in hostile encounters.* In order to win this battle that you are in for your future.

3.   YOU MUST BE SKILLED IN WARFARE.

Song of Solomon 3:8 says,

> "...they all hold swords, being experts in war (trained, ready for anything at any time) every man hath his sword upon his thigh because of fear in the night."

In order to become an expert at war you must have experience in being in many wars. Every battle you go through, improves your performance and will cause you to learn more about warfare!

You must have a high capacity for pressure, opposition and warfare. (Ex.: Paul in 2 Corinthians 11:23) Your combat is purposeful. *Combat is a fight or purposeful violent conflict.* The conflict you been in since birth is not without a cause. Combat weakens your enemy, it establishes dominance over the enemy, it kills your opposition instead of him killing you, and it drives the opposition away from where it is not wanted or needed. You don't need opposition in your life but the only way you're going to get it out is through combat. That was one of the children of Israel issues they didn't want to engage in combat. This is something I have learned is that if you stay in the fight no matter how long you will Win, why because the battle has already been won and it's rigged in your favor.

In warfare, there are four positions you can take, offence, defense, negotiation, or desertion and there is only one of them the enemy fears. Let's look at each position.

OFFENSE

Offense is *the act of attacking or assaulting, uncover and discern the plots, plans, tactics, and strategies of the enemy.* The bible says that God would not have us ignorant of Satan devices. It also means to move toward victory.

You must be in attack mode, and you must be intentional and deliberate about moving in victory. In order to move in victory, you must be calculating and strategic. The great thing about God is he will give you battle strategy. You are not fighting your battles alone. Don't always assume that every battle will be won the same way, always inquire of the Lord for strategy! Then you must trust the voice of The Lord, I repeat trust His voice! The children of Israel didn't trust the voice of God they allowed the giants to speak louder than God's voice. Voice is an idea of disclosure; every voice comes to disclose something to you. The bible says that there are so many kinds of voices (see 1 Corinthians 14:10) and you must be able to discern the different utterances and choose to follow the right voice. The other voices will lead you out of the will of God, but when you depend on and rely on God's voice it will cause you to come out victorious every time!

DEFENSE

Defense is defined as *resistance against the attacks, something that defends*. James 4:7 tells us *if we resist the devil he will flee*. You must resist the onslaughts of the enemy and be ready to defend the ground that you have already gained. Defense means you must protect where you are. Ephesians 6:11 says, "Put on the whole armor of God, that ye may be able to stand against the wiles of the devil." This is important because armor protects your vital organs. Know this you must protect your salvation, righteousness, faith, word, what you know to be truth, and your peace in the midst of the battle. These are all areas the enemy will oppose and attack.

NEGOTIATION

The word negotiation means *to compromise, to make a treaty or pact with the opposing side.*

If you are willing to negotiate that usually tells your enemies that you believe that they are more powerful than you are. Then they think they hold all the cards. It is in your weakest and most vulnerable times that the enemy will come to see if he can get you to compromise, just like he did with Jesus in Matthew chapter 4. Just like Jesus didn't compromise but used the word of God. When it comes to what God has said about your future you cannot, in any way, compromise or negotiate with your enemy either. You have to know that you hold all the power to defeat him.

DESERTION
Desertion is defined as *willful abandonment, act of leaving service or duty without the intention to returning.* The Bible says he that put his hand to the plow and looks back is not fit for the Kingdom (Luke 9:62). Satan's ultimate goal is to get you to

walk away from the Kingdom/God and never return. He wants to get you out from under your Shepherd that he may destroy you. No matter what you must stay the course and not give up willfully what's rightfully yours. Satan knows he can't legally take anything from you, but he can get you to abandon your purpose and promise. Don't forfeit, give up what rightfully belongs to you. As long as you continue to stand and keep pressing toward the mark you will reap in due season. Most of the time what happens is we give up when we're right there.

Let me encourage you that you're right at the brink of going into what God has for you. What you're about to experience is beyond your wildest dreams if you continue in the battle. Don't become battle weary! I decree that God will send Aaron's and Hur's (helpers) to hold your arms up until you get everything that God has ordained for your life before the foundations of the world!

As stated, there is only one of these positions the enemy fears and that is OFFENSE! When it comes to your future you must always be on the offence. Why because people that are on the offence knows that we aren't fighting for victory, but we fight from Victory! Fighting for victory implies that we are trying to get something that has already been given to us through Christ Jesus, whereas fighting from victory means we are protecting and keeping what we already have through Christ Jesus. We are a Victorious People!

1 Corinthians 15:57

> *"But thanks be to God, which giveth us the victory through our Lord Jesus Christ.*
>
> *Therefore, my beloved brethren, be ye stedfast, unmoveable, always abounding in the work of the Lord, forasmuch as ye know that your labour is not in vain in the Lord."*

This simply means that the battle is the Lord's and we live in the victory He has provided for us. Jesus has already defeated Satan, so you don't have to negotiate or compromise when it comes to your destiny. You can remain steadfast and not desert or abandon the life God has for you.

Through Christ Jesus your future is limitless, you can triumph over everything the enemy throws at you and enter into the place God has purposed and promised you!

I want to leave you with this: know that your life has been strategically planned out by God and He has a Designated Place, for a Designated Time and Season, with Designated People already assigned to your life that will help facilitate in your deliverance that will cause you to go Beyond! The word designate means to mark or point out, indicate, show, specify, to name, to nominate or select for duty or office, purpose, appoint, assign, and position.

POWER PRAYER

I declare that no confusion, nor the spirit of seduction would come to take you out of your position, I decree that you would be in the specific timing of God, you will not get behind or ahead of God, you will not miss the mark, I decree that you would know the office in which you have been appointed to and that every person that is assigned to your life would show up in the right times and seasons, In Jesus Name Amen!

I declare that this is your designated time for deliverance because you have been designated by God to go beyond to your designated place of purpose and promise!

MY POWER DECLARATIONS OVER YOU!

I prophesy that no matter what you've experienced or gone through, you shall no longer be bound, stuck or stagnant.

I declare that you're going to go further than you could ever think or imagine.

I declare that you will mount up with wings as eagles and you will soar!

I declare that you will leap over walls, and ever obstacle or opposition that has stood in your way!

I declare that you will not submit to any of the limitations-or restrictions, that may have been placed upon you by your past!

I declare there is nothing that is off limits!

I decree that you will go pass every feeling of being powerless!

I decree that you're going to explore every possibility and opportunity that is laid before you!

I declare that you will go beyond your past and access your future!

I break the powers of barrenness, being unfruitful, and being nonproductive off your life!

I decree that you will see God's best for you!

In Jesus Name, Amen!

www.ingramcontent.com/pod-product-compliance
Lightning Source LLC
LaVergne TN
LVHW051508070426
835507LV00022B/2992